new seasons®

New Seasons is a registered trademark of Publications International, Ltd.

Written by Holli Fort and Brandon Myers

Photography from: Shutterstock.com

Louis Weber, CEO
Publications International, Ltd.
8140 Lehigh Avenue
Morton Grove, IL 60053

www.pilbooks.com

Manufactured in China.

8 7 6 5 4 3 2 1

ISBN: 978-1-64558-372-1

Let's get social!

 @Publications_International

 @PublicationsInternational

www.pilbooks.com

HATS *on* CATS

I shall make your lap my throne.

Whoah, I had that snowboard dream again.

Of course I can fly.
I worked for Mewnited

Tabby Stylz owns casual Fridays.

Abracadabra, dog become a drooling furball. Hey, it worked!

Don't call me cute.
Call me a handsome devil.

Sorry, I already ate all the cream eggs.

Peace, love, and nose boops.

I'm ready to hit the beach.

I am a fully accredited member
of the purple bonkers hat society.

I will find your knitting
needles and deal with them.
Then I will deal with you.

Can someone please *steer* me in the right direction?

I'm definitely making this my profile picture.

My stage name is The Great Catsby,
but you can call me Jay.

Tabby or not tabby. That is the question.

I am the night, I am CATMAN!

Likes: going outside and coming back inside.
Also: going back outside.

Power nap #4 today.

Where does it hurt? Great, I'll sit there.

Get ready for the mane event!

Siesta: a word to you, an art form to me.

Strike a pose?
Darling, I've purrfected that art!

To hunt the reindeer,
I must become the reindeer.

The routine went well,
but I should have used
more jazz paws.

I find your reaction to my exploration
of the ventilation ducts excessive.

Ever had one of those days where you just feel like a tiny kitten in a fedora? Wait . . .

Ready for vacation—Canary Islands, here I come!

Today's lecture will cover
the theory and practice of
knocking things off ledges
for no reason.

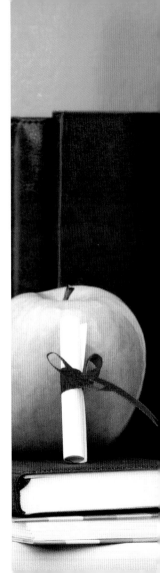

They can take my catnip but they can't take my knit cap.

You can't beat me. I'm Tomcat Brady.

I love the sea air, it smells like dinner.

It's not murder unless they find the feathers.

I'm a smitten kitten!
Will you be my valentine?

The catspiracy goes deeper than I thought.

Sir Nap-a-lot.

Not only that, I was wearing my birthday suit when they took the picture.

Meow you doin'?

C'mon, Mom, just five more minutes!

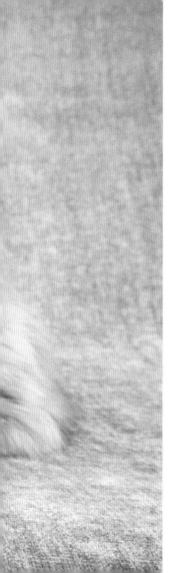

Laugh now, human,
but what has been seen
cannot be unseen.

The better to hear you with.

Season's greetings
to you from me.
I knocked this shiny thing
off your tree.

The forecast calls for a nap under the couch followed by light flurries of toe biting.

I want YOU—
to stop making me wear hats.

Purrple is my signature color.

Now for my next trick.
You've seen rabbits pulled from hats, but
have you seen dogs framed for breaking lamps?

Catitude is everything
in this business.

Wear the birdie hat, they said.
No one will laugh, they said.

My flowers are great, but you should taste my aspurragus and peppurrs.

I'm headed west, where the buffalo roam and baths are optional.

Safety first.

Let's just say the feather was wild-sourced.

They'll never spot me in this eggcellent disguise.